AF229275

NO SMART ANSWERS!

CARTOONS
by
Ghi Dean

Foreword by Lynn Johnston

First published by PINECREST PRESS,
Ancaster, Ontario, in 1987.

NO SMART ANSWERS
Teaching cartoons

by: Ghi Dean

ISBN: 0-921707-01-0

Published by:
First edition: 1987: Pinecrest Press, Ancaster, Ontario
Second edition: 2018: Createspace.com

Canadian Cataloguing in Publication Data

Dean, Ghi, 1944 -
No Smart Answers

ISBN: 0-921707-01-0
1. Teaching - Caricatures and Cartoons
2. Canadian wit and humour, Pictorial.
3. Title

NC1763.T39D43 1987 781.5'971 C87-09481-0

Foreword by Lynn Johnston

To my Dad

ABOUT THE AUTHOR

Even before Ghi Dean came to Canada at the age of eight, she was drawing houses, boats, people and pets. She first studied art at Hamilton's Delta Collegiate, where she met her future husband. After high school, she set aside her art studies until 1969 when she completed university and married. She started teaching French then and found she could use her sketching to keep her students' interest during class. When other teachers realized Ghi's artistic bent, she was asked to help illustrate a French series of texts and other teaching materials.

She spent four years in the classroom, then took time off to nurture her three children. To maintain her sanity and sense of humour, she developed **THE HOME FRONT**, a cartoon that was published in the Burlington Gazette.

Ghi went back to teaching after the children were in school and created flash cards for her French classes. Ghi exorcised the frustrations encountered in the classroom by lampooning teaching.
NO SMART ANSWERS contains the fruits of these efforts. There are situations depicted on these pages that every teacher experiences, and some of the solutions that many of us have used or dreamt of using.

FOREWORD

A couple of years ago, Ghi Dean sent me a package of cartoons. I often get packages of work from folks who want to be cartoonists, but Ghi's work was different. It was funny.

Right away, I sensed a kindred spirit, another soul like me, a mother who stalked the under-brush of household jungledom with a sense of humour - the ultimate tool for survival.

Over the phone, we commiserated. Over coffee we became friends. Ghi's insights into "the life of a teacher" are worth sharing, and I know you'll enjoy this, the second edition. It's about time this girl exposed herself in public.

Good luck, Dearie!

Lynn Johnston

ACKNOWLEDGEMENTS

A sincere 'thank you' to all my friend and relatives who helped to keep me going during the various stages of this book.

A special thanks to my husband *Doug*, who put up with a l lot.

Extra special thanks also to *Edie Summers*, for her valuable input and ever present support

A super "thank you" to Lynn Johnston for helping me to believe in myself.

A very special thank you to Max Coderre for believing in me.

And last but not least, thanks again Chris!

Ghi Dean

HI MISS, WHY
ARE YOU WEARING
YOUR PYJAMAS?

WHY ARE YOU
WEARNG YOUR
UNDERWEAR?

....TROUBLE SITTING IN CHAIRS?

I'M SORRY, SIR, BUT WE <u>DID</u> POST IT ON OUR BULLETIN BOARD.

AREN'T CHA S'POSED T'ACCEPT MY ANSER SO I DON'T GET DISCURIGED?

...IT'S ONE AND A HALF RIGHT...

YOU HAVE TO **START** SOMETHING BEFORE YOU CAN QUIT IT.

THAT BOY I SENT TO THE OFFICE?... HIS NAME IS TOMMY TRUMPER, **NOT** FREDDIE FRANKLIN

THINK OF HOW OFTEN THE WEATHERMAN IS WRONG, BUT **HE** KEEPS TRYING!

GROUP WORK: WHERE
FOUR KIDS USE
TWICE THE TIME TO DO
HALF THE WORK...

HERE ARE MY
NOTES, SIR.
SPORT
GHI
©G.Dean, 2018

Lesson 6
Test today.
DOES IT
COUNT ?
©G.Dean, 2018
GHI

BUT IT MIGHT
INHIBIT HIS
CREATIVE DEVELOPMENT...

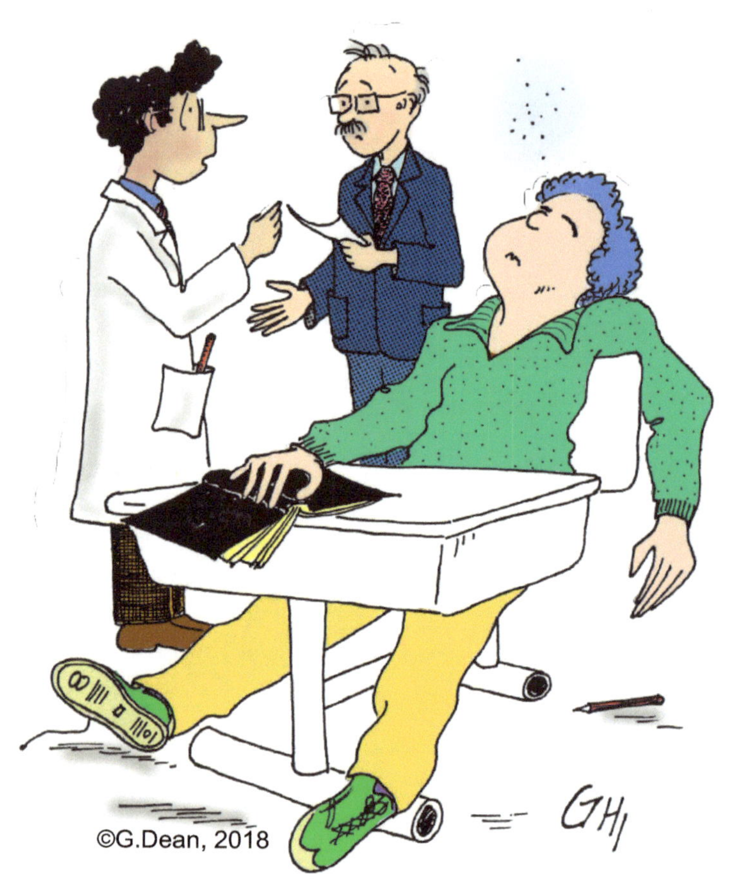

HE'S ONLY HERE UNTIL
HE FINDS A JOB!

THE "INSPECTOR"
MUST BE
COMING...
©G.Dean, 2018
GH

HI, SIR!
THIS IS MY FATHER...

AND SO ... AS I WAS SAYING .....

OK....SO... HOW LONG WOULD YOU LAST ON THE FOOTBALL TEAM IF YOU SENT **SOMEONE ELSE** TO PRACTICE FOR YOU?

WHY DO **OTHER TEACHERS**
GET ALL THE GOOD KIDS?

DO YOU PREFER TO BE CALLED "STRAWBERRY" OR "SHORTCAKE?"

IF FREDDIE REFUSES TO SEE THE PSYCHIATRIST AGAIN TODAY, CAN I HAVE HIS APPOINTMENT?

DISCIPLINE REPORT
The boy next to me wuz traving spitballs so I only ast him tu stop. I din't now why I got sent to the ofis maybe the teachurs having a bad day toda
Fred
he kicked the notebook, it flew high in the air, and the pages rained down on the front half of the classroom.
D. Baines.
GHI
©G.Dean, 2018

STILL LOOKING FOR YOUR GRADE FIVE TEACHER?
Classified
BIRTHS
DEATHS
GHI

©G.Dean, 2018
JOHN CAN GET HIS
PENCIL AFTER CLASS!
GH

FRENCH

WE
RE-CYCLE
REPORT
F
HEY! DON'T
WORRY - WE
RECYCLE TOO!
GH
©G.Dean, 2018

WE'RE GRATEFUL FOR THE OPPORTUNITIES THE NEW COMPUTERS OFFER TO OUR STUDENTS, SIR ... BUT....

PRE-DISCIPLINARY CHECKLIST
— DID YOU CHECK FOR:
- RECENT DEATH IN FAMILY.
- CHILD ABUSE.
- EMOTIONAL PROBLEMS.
- LEARNING DISABILITIES.
- HIDDEN FRUSTRATIONS.
- DID YOU GIVE THE STUDENT ENOUGH CHANCES?
- CAN THE SCHOOL AFFORD TO LOSE THE GRANT?
- COULD YOU BE THE PROBLEM?
©G.Dean, 2018
GH

I'VE BEEN IN FLORIDA
FOR 6 WEEKS, SIR.
DID I MISS ANYTHING?

©G.Dean, 2018
REMEMBER WHEN
CLASS TIME WAS
SACRED?
LOCKER
CLEAN-OUT
TODAY
PERIOD ONE

BECAUSE YOU'RE SUPPOSED TO BE LISTENING TO ME, THAT'S WHY!

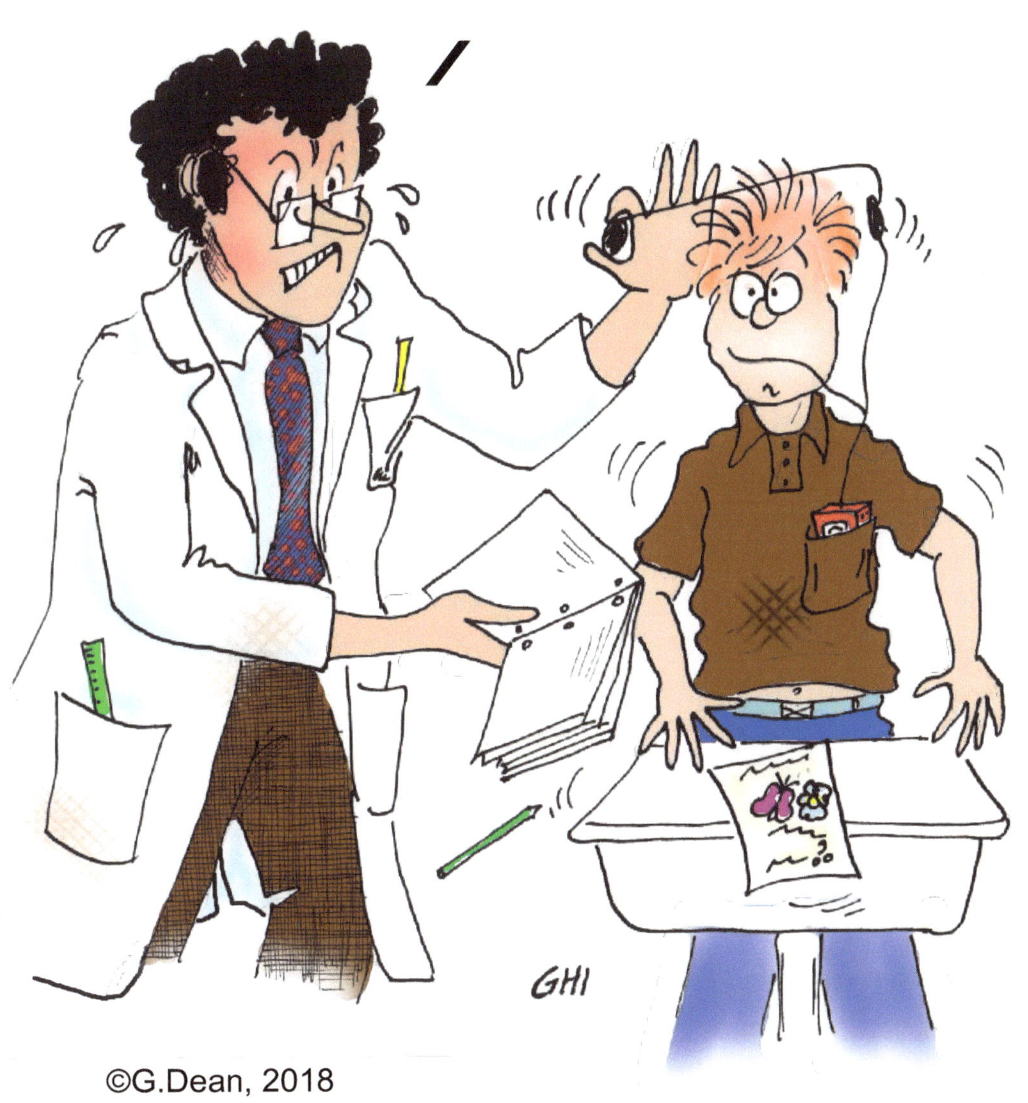

WE'RE
ON PAGE 84,
EXERCISE B,
NUMBER 6.
WE'RE ON
PAGE 48,
EXERCISE D,
NUMBER 9
©G.Dean, 2018
GHI

GOOD MORNING TOM.

GOOD MORNING, SIR.

XYZ 123

MACHO 1

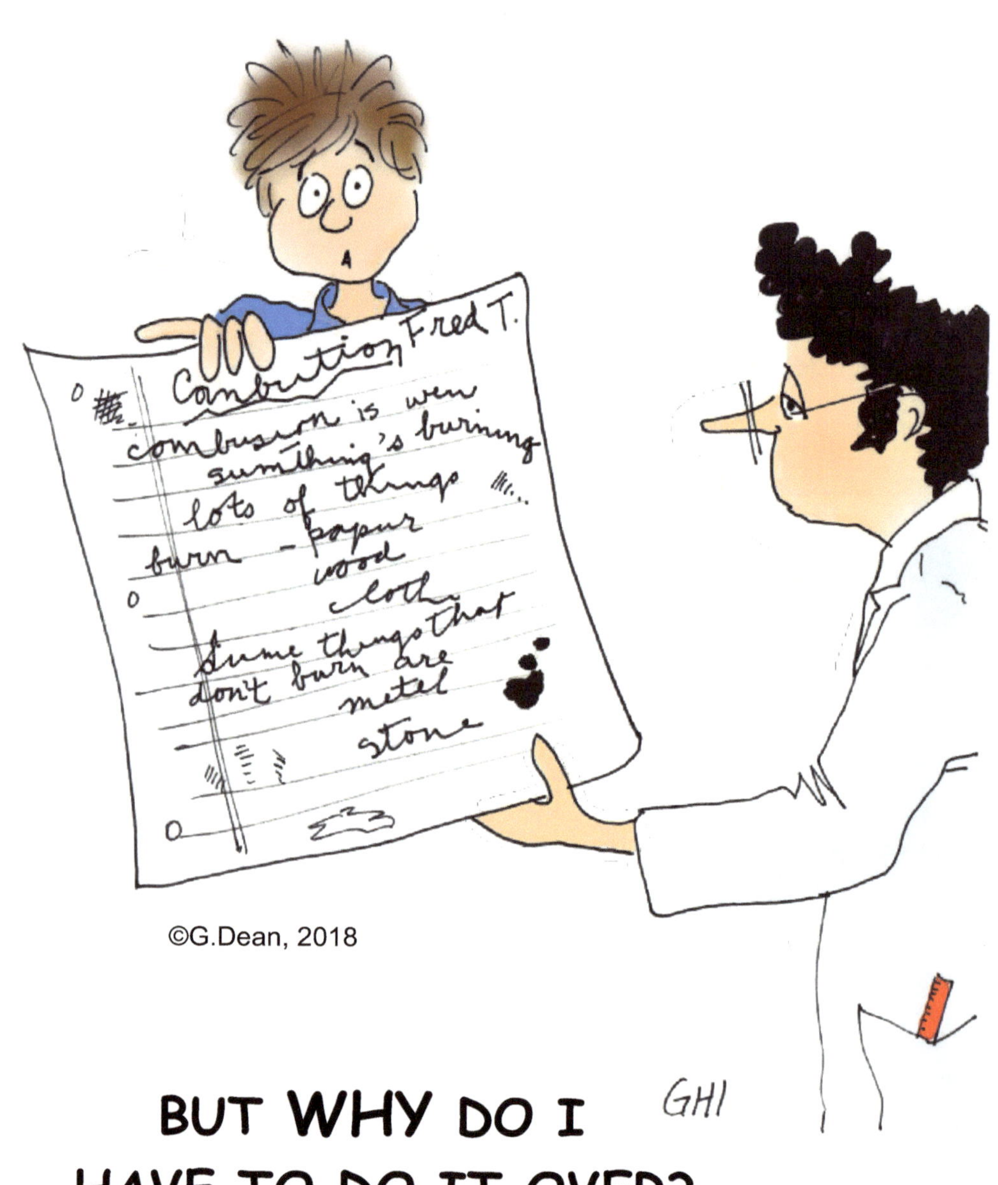

BUT WHY DO I HAVE TO DO IT OVER?

IF ONLY THEIR GUM 'D GLUE THEIR MOUTHS SHUT!
YAKKITY
YAK
YAP
BLA
BLABITY
YIP

HAPPY BIRTHDAY
MRS BAINES!
©G.Dean, 2018
GHI

IF YOUR METHOD OF PERSUASION DOESN'T WORK, CAN WE USE ONE OF OUR OWN?
METHODOLOGY WORKSHOP

GHI

OUT OF ORDER
EAT RATS
TEST
©G.Dean, 2018

THEY THINK THE COPIER'S ON THE BLINK!

ONLY 5 MORE MINUTES
FOR THIS EXERCISE, CLASS.

SESAME STREET TAUGHT HER
SHE CAN BE WHATEVER SHE WANTS,
BUT THEY DIDN'T TELL HER SHE
HAS TO WORK FOR IT.

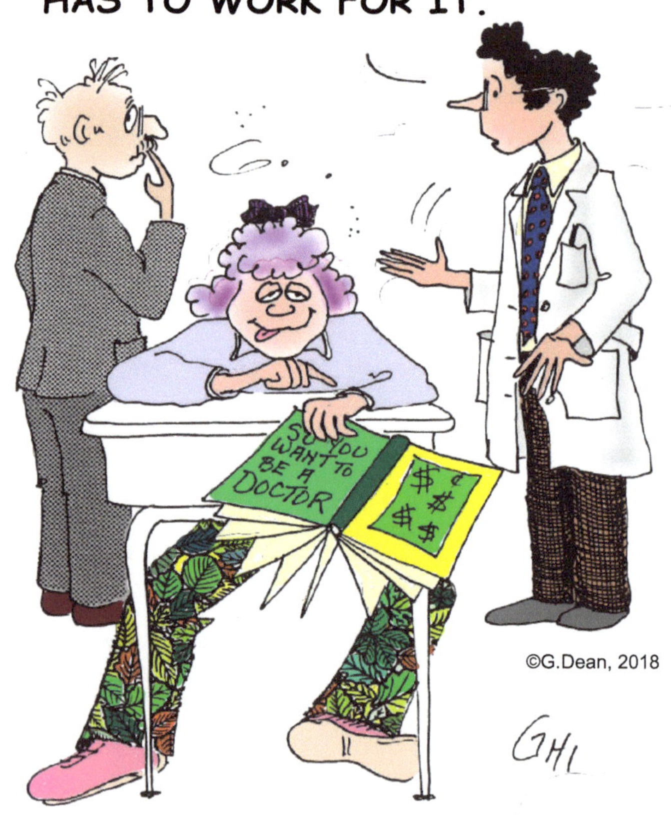

BUT MY MOM WON'T LET ME WATCH THE HOUSE OF COMMONS ON TV ANYMORE...

MISS, CAN WE PLAY GAMES?

WOW! FREDDIE'S DAD SURE DID A GREAT JOB ON THIS ONE!

ALL I SAID WAS:
"WORK ON YOUR
PROJECTS"

WHEN I SEND YOU TO THE OFFICE, BOYS, YOU'RE SUPPOSED TO GO IN
SCHOOL OFFICE
GHI
©G.Dean, 2018

SO, WHAT'S THIS THING ABOUT MY MOM GETTING A "LETTER OF CONCERN" ABOUT ME?
INTERIM REPORTS DUE...
GHI

AIN'T NUTHIN' YA CIN LEARN ME, AN I CIN QUIT ANYTIME, 'CAUSE I'M FIFTEEN AWREADY.

... I'LL HAVE MY SECRETARY MAKE AN APPOINTMENT FOR ME TO HAVE BREAKFAST WITH FREDERICK NEXT WEEK...

IS SHE A PROBLEM BECAUSE
SHE'S OUT OF HER OWN HOME,
OR
IS SHE OUT OF HER OWN HOME
BECAUSE SHE'S A PROBLEM?

OK, CLASS, THIS IS A TEST!
IS IT OPEN BOOK?
CAN WE LISTEN TO OUR WALKMANS?
BUT YOU NEVER TOLD US!
BUT PETE 'N ME NEVER WORK ALONE!
CAN WE WORK IN TEAMS?
DOES SPELLING COUNT? HISTORY? DATES?
CAN I DO MINE IN PENCIL? TOMORROW?
©G.Dean, 2018
GHI

tee
Bop
Bop
tee
bop...
Tap
©G.Dean, 2018
GHI

YOU TELL THEM TO HEAT THE WATER IN THE TEST TUBE UNTIL IT, BOILS, AND THEY WAIT FOR THE TEST TUBE TO BOIL...

GRADE 9: FREDDIE　　**GRADE 12: FRED, SIR**

WE DON' DO MEM'RY WORK.
NO HOME-WORK
WON'T BRING BOOKS TO CLASS!
NO DEADLINES!
YOU DO OUR NOTES!
NO TESTS!!
NO DETEN-TIONS!
GHI

LOOK, MISS, I GOT ALL MY ASSIGNMENTS DONE!
REPORTS
©G.Dean, 2018
CAN YOU MARK THEM RIGHT AWAY?
GHI

ISN'T THERE <u>ANYTHING</u>
I COULD DO TO PASS?

3 O'CLOCK AND ALL'S WELL...
Beep Bip!
Beep!
Beep!
Beep! Beep!
Beep!
Beep!
Beep!
Bip!
Bip! bip!
GHI

NOT ONE KID
ASKED TO LEAVE
THE ROOM TODAY

GEE ... WAS
ANYBODY THERE?

GHI

SCIENCE PROJECT
DUE
MONDAY
WHEN'S THE SCIENCE PROJECT DUE, SIR?
GHI

I'LL WASH THOSE UP FOR YOU, SIR!
GH
©G.Dean, 2018

GIVING DETENTIONS IS TOO JUVENILE FOR HIGH SCHOOL.
NEEDING A DETENTION IS TOO JUVENILE FOR HIGH SCHOOL.
GHI

Can I go to the bathroom?
Can we go to my locker?
FEEL FREE TO ASK ME ANY QUESTIONS...
Can I go meet my friends?
May I go for a drink?
C'n I go to the library?
I need to borrow a pen ...
I forgot my lunch ... c'n I go get it?
TEST TODAY.
Can I go talk to my geography teacher?
©G.Dean, 2018
Can I go to the drugstore?
GH1

SPRING SHOWERS
Book
Do not disturb
Snake sleeping
Nature Projects.

GIVE BLOOD
GO HOME.
NURSE
BLEED YOU SAP!
BLOOD DONOR CLINIC PERIOD 4 TODAY.
THEY DO
ANYTHING TO GET
OUT OF CLASS!
GHI

©G.Dean, 2018
WHY DON'T THEY MAKE DESKS WITH SEATBELTS?
BOOKS
BOOK

HEY, MISS, CAN I GO AND STAND IN THE HALL THIS PERIOD?

Français.

p146

Err....
True?
Um
False?
Uh...
False?
True ?
True?
Tralse?
False ?
PINK
SCHMUK
©G.Dean, 2018
GHI

YOU'RE SUPPOSED
TO BRING A PEN
EVERY DAY,
FREDERICK!
DICTIONNAIRE
DE FRANÇAIS
SCHEDULE
BULLETINS
©G.Dean, 2018

KEEP TRYING, AND BEFORE YOU KNOW IT YOU'LL **KNOW** IT!

HOW DID HE
DIE, SIR?
GHI
©G.Dean, 2018

CAN'T YOU WAIT 'TIL THE PERIOD'S OVER?

YOU REALLY DID IT THIS TIME, SIR! YOU GOT ME SUSPENDED!!!
GHI
©G.Dean, 2018

YOU KNOW WHO CAME?
... ONLY THE PARENTS OF THOSE WHO DON'T NEED HELP TO PASS......

STOP QUITTING!
GHI
©G. Dean, 2018

YOU WERE SUPPOSED TO
READ IT, FREDERICK!

THINK OF THE TEACHER WHO
GETS HIM NEXT TERM
IF YOU FAIL THIS KID.

... AS SOON AS WE GET THE HANG OF SOMETHING, **YOU** GO ON TO SOMETHING NEW...

I'M SORRY, SIR, MY CLASSROOM IS FULL!
OPTION SHEET
222
MATHS
GHI
©G.Dean, 2018

JUST YOU WAIT
UNTIL I'M A
TRUSTEE !

IT'S AGAINST MINISTRY POLICY TO MAKE LIFE EASIER FOR TEACHERS...
!
GH
©G.Dean, 2018

JUST GIVE HIM ONE MORE CHANCE, JUDY !

EXTRA WORK
YOUR BONUS IS THE SATISFACTION OF A JOB WELL DONE !
GHI
©G.Dean 2018

GHI
©G.Dean, 2018

AND BY THE END OF THE TERM, YOU'LL ALL BE **PERFECT** LIKE **ME** !

IF THE HOCKEY COACH REALLY **WANTS** YOU, HE CAN COME AND GET YOU!!!

HOW DID SHE KNOW?

3 SHOTS
AT THE
PRINCIPAL
$5.00
GHI

IT'S NOT SO MUCH **MY** FAILURE RATE AS IT IS **YOURS.**

THE RE-TEST IS NEXT YEAR!

BOO!

SEX
I hate FRENCH
MOM
Teachers are SICK

Thanks
for teaching
us, Mrs Baines
Kim
& Sue
©G.Dean, 2018
©G.Dean'85
GHI

OKAY ... WHO TURNED OFF THE LIGHTS???
GHI

Also by Ghi Dean (pen name Chris Williams) a novel about a teacher for one semester in a high school: *Behind the Teacher's Desk.*
<u>*(5 stars)*</u>

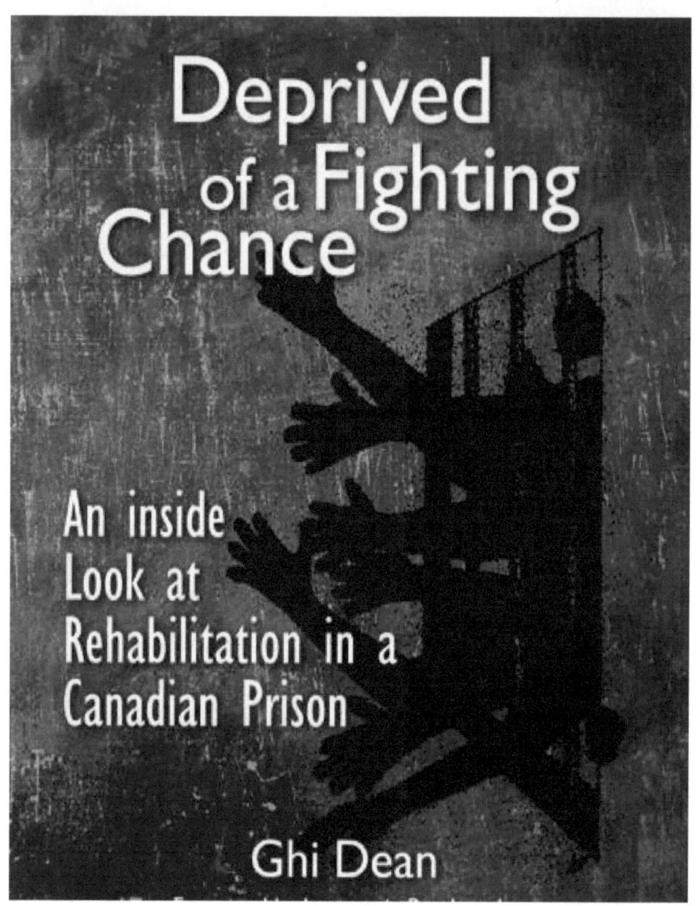

On a more serious note, her experiences working as education coordinator for adults in a maximum security detention centre. (5 stars) in *Deprived of a Fighting Chance.*

Also by Ghi Dean on a fun and educational note, her Fish for French series of card games. All illustrated by Ghi.

www.ingramcontent.com/pod-product-compliance
Lightning Source LLC
Chambersburg PA
CBHW041221050726
47599CB00001B/22

* 9 7 8 0 9 2 1 7 0 7 0 1 1 *